Can you find
Jim's hotel room?

 Are all the rooms the same as Jim's?

● How many rooms can you see?

Jim plays on the beach.

He makes a big sandcastle.

He puts a little green flag on top.

☆ Can you find all these shapes in the picture?

one big and one little square

one big and three
small round shapes

two big and two
small triangles

Jim and his friends go fishing
in the rock pools.
Look at the water-skiers.
They go very fast
and make big waves.

☆ Can you spot a crab, two seagulls, five
shells and Jim's flip-flops?

- Things moving on water leave a trail called a wake. How many wakes can you see?
- Spot the difference between the water-skiers.

Help!
The big waves
knock everyone over.
Jim and Jam fall into the sea.

☆ The anglers quickly pull their lines out of the water. Which angler has caught a fish? Which one got the boot?

- Where are the crab, seagulls, shells and flip-flops now?

The people in the boat
throw a lifebelt to Jim and Jam.
They come to rescue them.
They take everybody
back to the sandy beach.

☆ Some fishermen have put nets in the water.
How will the boat get past them back to the
sandy beach?

- Trace the way the boat should go with your finger.
- What shape are the floats on the nets?
- Are all the floats the same colour?

Jim and all his friends
put on their armbands.
Then they will be safer
in the water.

☆ Can you find the matching armband
   for each child?

- Can you tell which person is flying which kite?
- What shape are the kites?

An ice cream
makes everybody feel better.
Goodbye Jim! Goodbye Jam!

☆ Can you match the children's ice creams
with the pictures on the poster?

- How many children had a drink as well as an ice cream?
- Which ice cream would you like?

Word and Picture Puzzle

bucket

water-skier

boat

spade

seagull

shell

ball

flip-flops

sea

rock

sandcastle

kite

Look at these pictures and read the words several times.
Try putting a strip of paper (or a coin, or your hand)
over the pictures. Now can you read what each word says?

Sea Rescue!

Here is a game to play alone or with friends. Fill a washing-up bowl with water, and float on it some 'boats' made from foil cake cases or plastic lids (or make some from kitchen foil). Find some little toy people to be sailors. Then blow hard under the water through your straw, and make a terrible storm. Lots of your boats will capsize – so rescue your sailors with a lifebelt! Make this by cutting a ring from an empty plastic bottle, or use a plastic bracelet. Hang your lifebelt from a piece of string. The player who rescues most sailors wins.

Make a Beachcomber Picture

You will need

 children's glue

 cardboard box lid

 dry sand

 sticky tape

 string

 treasures from the beach

First, cover the table you are going to work on with some old newspapers to keep it clean. Then spread some children's glue all over the inside of a cardboard box lid. Cover this thickly with dry sand. When the glue is dry, shake off any extra sand on to the newspaper. Now you have a beach on to which you can stick all the treasures you have found. Fix a loop of string to the back of the lid with sticky tape, and hang up your picture.

Make a Shell Paperweight

You will need

 shells

plastic lid of yoghurt or margarine tub

 plaster of Paris

water

teacup

 bowl and spoon

Remember – have everything ready before you start! Measure out about half-a-teacup of plaster of Paris, and tip it into a bowl. Slowly add water (about two tablespoonsful), stirring until the mixture looks like very thick cream. Pour it into the shallow well of your plastic lid (and quickly rinse out your bowl and spoon with lots of water). While the plaster in the lid is still soft, press into it any pretty shells or pebbles that will fit. When the plaster has set hard, cut a slit in the edge of the lid and peel it away from the plaster cast. Now your shell paperweight is ready to use.

Lighthouse Game

finish

A game for two people. You will need a dice, and two counters. Choose your lighthouse and put your counter on its door. Take turns to throw the dice, and move your counters up the coloured and white stripes of the lighthouse. First lighthouse keeper to reach his yellow light is the winner!

finish

start here

start here